When Dad Hurts Mum

Sheila Hollins, Patricia Scotland and Noëlle Blackman
illustrated by Anne-Marie Perks

Beyond Words

London

2

4

11

14

15

16

20

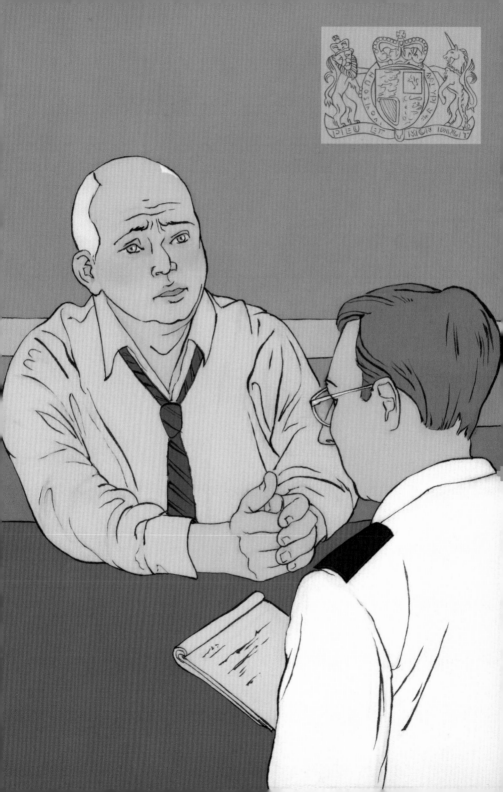

First edition published 2014 by Books Beyond Words.

Text & illustrations © Books Beyond Words 2014.

ISBN 978-1-78458-036-0

British Library Cataloguing-in-Publication Data
A catalogue record for this book is available from the British Library.

Printed by Advent Print Group, Andover.

Books Beyond Words is a Community Interest Company registered in England and Wales (7557861).

St George's Hospital Charity is a registered charity (no. 241527).

Contents

Storyline

The following words are provided for readers and supporters who want some ideas about one possible story. Most readers make their own story up from the pictures.

1. Joseph comes home for a visit. Mum's at the door to say hello.

2. Joseph hugs his sister Katie. She's happy to see him.

3. Katie and Joseph have dinner with Mum and Dad. Dad looks angry about something.

4. Dad points and shouts at Mum, and Mum is frightened. Katie and Joseph want him to stop.

5. Dad slaps Mum in the face. She cries out. He's hurt her and she's very frightened.

6. Katie sits on her own on the stairs. She listens to what's happening downstairs.

7. Dad leaves the house. Joseph shouts at him, "We don't want you here!" He tries to comfort Mum, too. She's crying and her face is sore.

8. Everyone's upset. Katie and Mum are crying. Joseph hugs Katie and comforts her.

9. Joseph says goodbye. He's sad to leave Mum and Katie on their own.

10. Katie goes to college. She still thinks about what happened. She feels sad.

11. Katie's in class. Her friend Anne is working, but Katie doesn't do any work. She worries about Mum and Dad. The teacher sees.

12. It's lunchtime. Katie's friends chat, but Katie doesn't feel like talking. Katie's teacher worries about her.

13. Katie's teacher tries to talk to her. She wants to find out why Katie is sad. It's hard for Katie to talk about her parents.

14. The teacher has brought some books for Katie to look at. Maybe one of the books will help.

15. They sit down and look at one of the books together. Katie finds a picture she wants to talk about. She tells the teacher what happened at home. The teacher listens carefully.

16. There's a meeting at college. Katie, Mum and the teacher are there. There is another woman there to help them, called Brenda. Mum feels nervous. She has a black eye now.

17. Katie points at Mum's black eye. "Why did he hurt you?" They are both upset.

18. Mum talks to Brenda on her own now. She tells Brenda what happened at home.

19. Brenda and Mum ring the police together.

20. Dad is under arrest. What he did to Mum was against the law.

21. Dad's at the police station now. The police officer asks him about what he did.

22. A police officer brings Dad home to pack up his things. He can't stay at home now.

23. Dad's in court. The magistrates will decide what happens if he is guilty. Brenda's there too to hear what they decide.

24. Dad's in a group for men. One man tells his story. He did something bad, too. The other men listen. They want to learn how to stop hurting women.

25. Dad feels upset and guilty about what he did. "Why did I do it?"

26. Brenda comes to visit Katie and Mum. She tells them what has happened to Dad. Brenda can help Mum and Katie stay safe and find support.

27. Joseph comes for a visit. Mum and Katie are happy to see him. Joseph has brought a surprise for Katie. It's a kitten!

28. Katie, Mum and Joseph sit down together for dinner. The kitten's there too. They are all safe and happy. Dad doesn't live there any more.

What is domestic abuse?

Domestic abuse is the name given to abuse between people who are in, or have been in, an intimate or family-type relationship.

Domestic abuse is when one person in a relationship tries to dominate and control the other person through threats, violence or other abuse. It can take the form of physical, psychological, sexual or financial abuse, and forms a pattern of bullying and controlling behaviour. This can also include forced marriage and so-called 'honour' crimes. Domestic abuse that includes physical violence is sometimes called domestic violence.

Domestic abuse is very common and can happen in both heterosexual and same-sex partnerships. It can happen to people of all ages, ethnic backgrounds, and economic levels. And while women are more commonly victims of domestic abuse, it can happen to men, too.

Growing up in a family where there is domestic abuse can leave a young person with painful and overwhelming emotions of guilt, betrayal and rejection. It can have a considerable impact on how they grow up and form their own relationships. Sometimes people who have grown up in a home where there is domestic abuse later enter into intimate relationships which become abusive. This may be because some of the behaviour that is abusive has come to seem normal to them. Domestic abuse can have a long-lasting and damaging effect on everyone involved.

What is not safe in a relationship?

Abusive behaviour is never acceptable, whether it's coming from a man, a woman, a teenager, or an older adult.

The abuse can take the form of emotional abuse, which could include verbal abuse such as yelling, name-calling, blaming, and shaming. It can also be controlling behaviour, such as isolating the person or frightening them with threats. The abuse can escalate from threats and verbal abuse to violence. And while physical injury may seem the most obvious danger, the emotional and psychological consequences of domestic abuse are serious and long-lasting. Emotionally abusive relationships can destroy a person's self-worth, and can lead to anxiety and depression, making the person feel helpless and alone.

Below is a list of the kinds of behaviour that would be considered to be domestic abuse:

- disrespect: regular criticism; persistently putting the person down in front of other people or embarrassing them in public; not listening or responding when they talk; interrupting telephone calls

- verbal abuse: shouting; mocking; accusing; name-calling; verbally threatening

- use of pressure tactics: sulking; threatening or attempting suicide; threatening to make reports to agencies unless the person gives in to the abuser's demands

- removing choice and power: telling the other person that they have no choice in any decisions; lying or withholding information; withholding or pressuring the person to use drugs or other substances; withholding money or taking money from the person's purse without asking; taking the children away; refusing to take any part in helping with childcare or housework

- isolating: telling the other person where they can and cannot go; preventing them from seeing friends and relatives; shutting the person in the house; lying to the person's friends and family about them; monitoring or blocking telephone calls or disconnecting the telephone; being unreasonably jealous; having other relationships; breaking promises and shared agreements

- harassment: following or checking up on the other person; not allowing any privacy (for example, opening mail); checking to see who has telephoned the other person; accompanying them everywhere they go

- physical threats: making angry gestures; using physical size to intimidate; shouting the other person down; destroying the other person's possessions; breaking things; punching walls; wielding a knife or a gun; threatening to kill or harm the other person and/or the children; threatening to kill or harm family pets

- sexual violence: using force, threats or intimidation to make the other person perform sexual acts; having sex with the other person when they don't want it; forcing them to look at pornographic material; forcing them to have sex with other people; any degrading treatment related to the other person's sexuality or gender, whether they are lesbian, gay, bisexual or heterosexual, or transgender

- physical violence: punching; slapping; hitting; biting; pinching; kicking; pulling hair out; pushing; shoving; burning; strangling

- denial: saying the abuse doesn't happen; saying the other person caused the abusive behaviour; being publicly gentle and patient; crying and begging for forgiveness; saying it will never happen again.

Growing up with domestic abuse

A parent who is suffering domestic abuse may try to protect their children from seeing the abuse or being affected by it, but around 750,000 children a year in the UK will see or hear domestic abuse or be aware of the physical or emotional results of it. Sometimes young people will want to protect a parent, or they may end up having to deal with the consequences of abuse, for example taking a parent to hospital if they are badly hurt. In the worst cases children become direct victims of the abuse alongside their parent.

Growing up in a household where domestic abuse is taking place will have profound and painful emotional effects on young people. Children may feel powerless or guilty about what is happening to their parent; they may be angry with either parent, or suffer fear, anxiety, depression and sleeplessness. Domestic abuse makes a child or young person's home unsafe and can change how they feel about both parents.

It can be very difficult for children and young people to talk about domestic abuse. It may be something that is not spoken about within the home, and that becomes a 'family secret' outside the home. Some young people may fear losing their family if the abuse becomes known. However, if you know a child or young person well, or work with them, for example as a teacher, some aspects of their behaviour may make you suspect serious problems at home:

- withdrawing or appearing anxious or depressed

- avoiding friends; not inviting friends home

- tiredness, lack of appetite or physical symptoms, such as tummy ache or bed-wetting

- temper tantrums or aggression

- difficulties at school, lack of concentration, low attainment or truancy

- developmental delays, such as speech disorders, in younger children

- eating disorders or self harm, alcohol or substance abuse in older children

It takes a huge amount of bravery for a young person to talk about domestic abuse, but breaking the silence is the first step in making sure that they and their parent can be kept safe. Young people who have experienced or witnessed domestic abuse will need the strong and lasting support of peers and adults whom they trust.

Safeguarding

Professionals working with children will have a safeguarding policy in their organisation stating how they should respond to a disclosure of abuse. If a child or young person tells you they have been a victim of abuse or that abuse is happening at home, you should listen with tact and believe what they tell you, and think about what to do with the information. Abuse cannot be kept a secret even if the child wishes, and it is important to be honest with them about what will happen next. Their safety is the most important concern. If a child or an adult at risk tells you that they are in danger or have suffered abuse, you should report it to the police or to the local authority social services department.

Reporting domestic abuse

Domestic abuse is a serious and violent crime. It is unacceptable and should not be tolerated. If you or someone you know is in immediate danger call 999. The police take domestic violence seriously and will be able to help and protect you or that person. If it is not an emergency but you want to find more support, you can contact your local neighbourhood policing team. If the police consider someone to be at risk (they should carry out a risk assessment), they will allocate a police liaison officer.

The police liaison officer's priority will be the person's safety, both now and in the future. As well as offering continued support and advice, they can help keep the person (and if necessary their children) free from abuse in a number of ways.

Independent Domestic Violence Advocates (IDVA) can also provide support and advice, allowing the police to concentrate on the investigation. An IDVA is a trained specialist whose goal is the safety of domestic abuse victims, focusing on victims at high risk of harm. The IDVA will work closely with the victim and all agencies involved in implementing the safety plan and supporting the victim through the criminal justice process.

In some areas there are also Children's Independent Domestic Violence Advocates (KIDVA), who are specially trained to support children who are victims of domestic abuse.

Below you'll find more detailed descriptions of some of the actions the police, IDVA and other agencies can take to keep the person safe.

- Sanctuary schemes: this is when a safe room is created in a person's own home, by fitting new doors, locks and lighting. The person can use the room to call the police and wait in safety.

- Safeguarding the home: a Crime Prevention Tactical Advisor will visit and look at what can be done to help keep the person safe.

- Home alterations: the police can work with local councils to get security alterations made to the person's home, for example changing locks and fitting strong doors.

- Mobile phones: police can provide new mobile phones if people need them to keep safe.

- Address marker: police can put a special marker on a person's address so they know to come as quickly as possible when a call is made.

- Safety plans: if someone is living with domestic abuse they can get support to make a personal safety plan. This will help the person plan in advance how they will leave their home in an emergency. Police or an IDVA can help the person think about an escape plan, such as packing an emergency bag, hiding it somewhere safe, and drawing up a list of emergency phone numbers to carry with them.

- Moving home: if the person is a council tenant and needs to move, the police or IDVA can liaise with the local council to arrange this. They can also put the person in contact with organisations who can help them (and, if necessary, their children) find a place at a refuge or safe house. Refuge addresses are always kept confidential.

- Support through court proceedings: if the abuser is taken to court, the police liaison officer or IDVA can talk the person through the court proceedings and arrange for them to give evidence behind a screen or via video link if they would prefer. If the person would rather not be in court, the police liaison officer or IDVA will make sure that they are told what happens.

What will happen to the victim and perpetrator once domestic abuse has been reported to the police?

Once a report has been made, the police's main concern will be the victim's safety. They will take what you say seriously, and respond quickly, especially if the domestic violence is occurring when you call. If you are a witness, police officers might ask you to give an oral and written account of what you heard or saw.

The perpetrator might be arrested, and then charged with a crime. Sometimes, the witness who called the police might be asked to come to court to testify about the events in front of the judge. If this is the case, the witness will be served with an official document, called a subpoena, which requests his or her presence at the court house at a specific date and time.

However, calling the police about domestic violence does not necessarily mean that you will need to testify in court. Quite often, due to other evidence or the perpetrator's confession, the witness does not have to appear.

Whatever the case may be, the simple act of calling the police about domestic abuse will clearly help to protect the victim, which is the most important thing. As a witness, you generally do not have to worry that the perpetrator will hurt you or the victim in revenge. There are services in place to protect you both.

When an incident of domestic abuse is reported, a police officer will visit the victim either at home or somewhere that they feel safe. The officer will talk to the victim about what has happened. Some of the questions may seem personal but the answers will really help the police to understand the situation and help to develop a plan in partnership with the person to keep them safe. The officer may also take a statement and will talk the victim through this step-by-step.

With the victim's permission the police may also gather other evidence such as medical records and take photographs of any injuries they may have.

The police also have a responsibility to make sure any children are kept safe, and will share information with social services so they can work to protect the victim and their family. The children will not be removed from the victim if they are not at risk from them.

If someone is arrested

Police officers take domestic abuse seriously. Although getting justice is important to them, officers consider each case and the wishes of people involved individually.

If someone is arrested they'll be taken to a police station. If they're charged with a crime, they may be remanded into custody to appear before the next available court or released on bail while the police complete their investigation. They may be able to attach bail conditions to protect the victim from further abuse and intimidation. The court may also use Domestic Abuse Protection Orders or Notices, which are civil orders that give the victim short-term protection from their abuser, enabling the victim to focus on making plans and sorting out necessary things like childcare or somewhere to live.

If the abuser pleads guilty the victim won't have to go to court but may be asked to give a victim impact statement describing the effect the abuse has had on them. The court will take this into account when passing sentence.

If the abuser pleads not guilty the victim may have to go to court to give evidence. This is likely to raise anxiety but arrangements can be made for the victim to do this behind a screen or via video link so that they don't have to enter the court room.

How can people keep safe in relationships?

One of the best ways to help people keep safe in relationships is to help them to build up their confidence and self-esteem. One way of doing this is through taking part in drama and role play. This is also a really good way for people to focus on thinking about how people relate to one another and to work out the difference between unhealthy and healthy relationships. Role play can offer people the opportunity to try out different ways of responding to different situations. This can be like a rehearsal so that it becomes easier to be assertive in real relationships.

Creating opportunities to talk about relationships and 'good' and 'bad' ways of treating one another are also really helpful. This can be done either in a small group or one to one. This book can be a good starting point to begin these kinds of discussions.

Therapy and counselling

Psychodynamic psychotherapy and counselling work through the therapeutic relationship which is built up between client and therapist. This can be particularly important for people who have experienced abusive intimate relationships all their lives. The therapeutic relationship becomes a first chance to experience a trusting, safe relationship, and it can become a useful part of helping to support someone to change their relationship patterns.

The therapy sessions also provide an opportunity for the person to discuss what is happening in their life, working out what is okay in their 'real life' relationships and what isn't, and to think about how they can bring about changes if they are unhappy with the way things are.

Useful resources

The Global Foundation for the Elimination of Domestic Violence (EDV)

EDV Global Foundation is an NGO working to end domestic violence worldwide. EDV works with international organisations and at a governmental level through a combination of education and advocacy to raise awareness of the problem, and a process of researching, designing and implementing programmes to tackle domestic violence in an effective way. EDV's website contains details of their work, and other news and policy developments relating to the elimination of domestic violence.

www.gfedv.org

Services in the UK

Social services

Social services are provided by the local authority to ensure that adults and children receive the support they need to live well. They are responsible for carrying out social care assessments, requesting funding if someone needs social care support, including supported living or emergency rehousing, and reviewing that support. They will also lead on safeguarding proceedings if an adult or child is at risk of harm or abuse.

Respond

Respond works with children and adults with learning disabilities who have experienced abuse or trauma, as well as those who have abused others, through psychotherapy, advocacy, campaigning and other support. Respond also provides training, consultancy and research to combat abuse.

Helpline: 0808 808 0700
www.respond.org.uk

Beverley Lewis House
Beverley Lewis House is a supported housing service run by East Thames Group that safeguards women with learning disabilities and mental health issues or physical disabilities, who are at risk of, or fleeing abuse. Accommodation is provided for up to two years, and during this time residents are given help and support to recover from their abuse, develop new skills and interests and build confidence. Women can be referred to Beverley Lewis House by their social worker.
www.east-thames.co.uk/sites/default/files/user/
images/Beverley%20Lewis%20House_brochure%20
%282%29.pdf

National Centre for Domestic Violence (NCDV)
A free national service to help people who have suffered or are threatened with domestic violence to get an emergency injunction. The NCDV will help prepare statements, arrange court appearances, and refer people to legal aid or provide volunteers to draft injunction applications.
0844 8044 999 / 0800 970 2070
Or text NCDV to 60777 to receive a call back
www.ncdv.org.uk

Women's Aid
Women's Aid is a national charity aiming to stop domestic abuse via campaigning, education and services to women suffering abuse. Local member organisations provide direct support and services, such as outreach, refuge accommodation and training for schools and organisations.

www.womensaid.org.uk
To find your local Women's Aid organisation, visit the national website:
www.womensaid.org.uk/azrefuges.asp

Refuge
Refuge is a national charity providing direct services to women experiencing domestic abuse, via a network of safe houses. Women, and their children, are supported to recover from their abuse while living in safety, and to access further services, including legal advice, education and employment and a safe place to live. A number of culturally specific refuges are provided. Refuge also provides Independent Domestic Violence Advocates (IDVAs) to work with women at high risk from their abusers.
www.refuge.org.uk

National Domestic Violence Helpline
The freephone 24-hour National Domestic Violence Helpline is run in partnership between Women's Aid and Refuge. The helpline can provide emotional support, information, and referrals to emergency safe accommodation and other services.
0808 2000 247

The ManKind Initiative
A national charity that provides help and support for male victims of domestic abuse. ManKind runs a helpline for men experiencing abuse, and works to raise awareness and provide training for organisations working with male victims of domestic abuse.
Helpline: 01823 334244
www.mankind.org.uk

Men's Advice Line

A helpline for men experiencing abuse from a partner, ex-partner or family member, offering emotional and practical support and signposting to other services. The website also provides tools for working with men who present as victims of domestic abuse.
Helpline: 0808 801 0327
www.mensadviceline.org.uk

Broken Rainbow

A national charity supporting lesbian, gay, bisexual and transgender victims of domestic abuse. Support is offered via a free confidential helpline, email and online chat.
Helpline: 0800 999 5428
Monday and Thursday 10am–8pm;
Tuesday and Wednesday 10am–5pm
help@brokenrainbow.org.uk
www.brokenrainbow.org.uk

Respect

A telephone and email service for people who are abusing their partners, offering support for them to stop. The website offers information about domestic abuse perpetrator programmes, and resources for working with domestic abuse perpetrators.
Respect phoneline: 0808 802 4040
Monday to Friday, 9am–5pm
info@respectphoneline.org.uk
www.respect.uk.net

Childline

Childline is a free 24-hour counselling service for children and young people up to 19. Counsellors can talk about any issue of concern, including domestic

abuse that young people are suffering or witnessing. Support is available via phone, or by instant message and email through the Childline website.
Helpline: 0800 1111
www.childline.org.uk

Get connected
A free confidential support and signposting service for young people under 25. The service offers support via telephone, text, email and webchat, covering a variety of issues including domestic abuse.
Helpline: 0808 808 4994
text: 80849
www.getconnected.org.uk

Victim Support
Victim Support is a national charity supporting people affected by crime, including domestic abuse. People can be referred by the police or can refer themselves whether or not they report the crime and regardless of when the crime happened. Victim Support also operates a confidential helpline.
Victim Supportline: 0845 30 30 900
Monday to Friday 8am–8pm; weekends 9am–7pm
www.victimsupport.org.uk

Rape Crisis
An organisation supporting women and girls who have been the victim of sexual violence, outside or within a relationship. Rape Crisis has a network of local centres offering services such as counselling, advocacy, training and outreach. A national helpline is also available.
Helpline: 0808 802 9999
www.rapecrisis.org.uk

Against Forced Marriages

An organisation raising awareness and supporting communities where people are at risk of forced marriage. There is a freephone helpline for anyone who has concerns about themselves or another person.
Helpline: 0800 141 2994
www.againstforcedmarriages.org
Any urgent cases should be reported to the government **Forced Marriage Unit (FMU)**.
FMU: 020 7008 0151

Written materials and online resources

A number of locally funded anti-domestic abuse projects have produced useful online resources. Below is a small selection.

Bristol Against Violence and Abuse (BAVA)

www.bava.org.uk
BAVA has produced a teaching pack and video resource aimed specifically at people with learning disabilities. The video features members of Misfits Theatre acting out different domestic abuse scenarios, with opportunities for viewers to reflect on and discuss what they are seeing.
www.bava.org.uk/professionals/resources
The Spiralling video and toolkit on the same page is aimed at young people.

Equation

www.equation.org.uk
The Equation Project, formerly Nottinghamshire Domestic Violence Forum, offers some good interactive resources for young people to learn about what makes healthy relationships, and to spot problems in their

own relationships or relationships around them. The GREAT Project is for children aged 9–11
www.thegreatproject.org.uk
Respect Not Fear is for young people aged 12–18
www.respectnotfear.co.uk

Can You See Me?

www.canyouseeme.coop
A video and educational resource produced by Women's Aid and the Midcounties Cooperative about relationships and abuse. There are resources and activities aimed at both young people and teachers, and a broad range of abusive behaviour is covered.

Easy Health

www.easyhealth.org.uk
An easy read website of resources about health and wellbeing topics, including abuse. All the linked leaflets and organisations are aimed at people with learning disabilities.

NICE public health guidance, *Domestic violence and abuse: how health services, social care and the organisations they work with can respond effectively*. This guidance sets out a number of recommendations for training and partnership working for services dealing with domestic violence.
www.nice.org.uk/guidance/ph50

Related titles in the Books Beyond Words series

Supporting Victims (2007) by Sheila Hollins, Kathryn Stone and Valerie Sinason, illustrated by Catherine Brighton. Polly is the victim of an assault. The book shows her experience as a witness at court, outlining the support and special measures that help her to give evidence.

Finding a Safe Place from Abuse (2014) by Sheila Hollins, Patricia Scotland and Noëlle Blackman, illustrated by Anne-Marie Perks. Katie meets David and falls in love. She moves in with him, but the relationship turns difficult and dangerous when David begins to steal her money and hurt her physically. Katie quickly gets help through her GP. After a stay in a refuge, Katie begins a new life with a new sense of confidence.

Jenny Speaks Out (2005, 2nd edition) by Sheila Hollins and Valerie Sinason, illustrated by Beth Webb. Jenny feels unsettled when she moves into a new home in the community. Her supporter and friends sensitively help Jenny to unravel her painful past as a victim of sexual abuse, and begin a slow but positive healing process.

Bob Tells All (1993) by Sheila Hollins and Valerie Sinason, illustrated by Beth Webb. Bob has moved to a group home, but his erratic behaviour and terrifying nightmares unsettle the other people living there. A social worker sensitively helps Bob unravel his painful past as a victim of sexual abuse. Bob discovers that talking with people he can trust begins a slow, but positive, healing process.

I Can Get Through It (2009, 2nd edition) by Sheila Hollins, Christiana Horrocks and Valerie Sinason, illustrated by Lisa Kopper. This book tells the story of a woman whose life is suddenly disturbed by an act of abuse. It shows how with the help of friends and counselling, the memory of the abuse slowly fades.

Mugged (2002) by Sheila Hollins, Christiana Horrocks and Valerie Sinason, illustrated by Lisa Kopper. This book tells the story of Charlie who is attacked in the street. The pictures show how Charlie is helped by speedy police action, Victim Support and back-up from friends, family and supporters.

Speaking Up For Myself (2002) by Sheila Hollins, Jackie Downer, Linette Farquarson and Oyepeju Raji, illustrated by Lisa Kopper. Having a learning disability and being from an ethnic minority group can make it hard to get good services. Natalie learns to fix problems by being assertive and getting help from someone she trusts.

Authors and artist

Sheila Hollins is Emeritus Professor of Psychiatry of Disability at St George's, University of London, and sits in the House of Lords. She is a past President of the Royal College of Psychiatrists and of the BMA, and chairs the BMA's Board of Science. She is founding editor, author and Executive Chair of Books Beyond Words, and a family carer for her son who has a learning disability.

Patricia Scotland, Baroness Patricia Scotland of Asthal QC was the first female Attorney General for the UK. She has achieved several firsts: in 1991 aged thirty-five, she became the youngest woman ever to be appointed Queen's Counsel and was the first black woman appointed to the House of Lords. She is a committed activist in matters pertaining to legal reform, domestic violence and criminal justice, and is patron of the Global Foundation for the Elimination of Domestic Violence.

Noëlle Blackman is CEO of Respond, a charity which provides psychotherapy to people with learning disabilities who have experienced abuse or trauma. She has co-facilitated the GOLD (Growing Older with Learning Disabilities) group since 1998, and uses Books Beyond Words in her therapeutic practice. This is the third book she has co-authored with Baroness Hollins.

Anne-Marie Perks is an illustrator, visual artist and animator with published work in children's books. She has an MA in Children's Illustration from the North Wales School of Art and Design. Her paintings have won awards in exhibitions in the US and she frequently shows her work in the Society of Children's Book Writers' and Illustrators' touring exhibitions. Anne-Marie teaches illustration and animation at Buckinghamshire New University.

Acknowledgments

We thank our editorial advisers Deborah Jamieson and Gary Butler.

We are grateful for the advice and support of our advisory group, which included representatives from Global Federation for the Elimination of Domestic Violence, Respond, Bromley Sparks, Beverley Lewis House, Tizard Centre, STORM Empowerment, Wandsworth Psychological Therapies & Wellbeing Service: John Phillips, Sylv Hibbit, Gillian Rees, Sue Langley, Jenny Cashman, Asha Jama, Michelle McGovern, Michelle McCarthy, Marie Hanson, Tina Cowles, Mavis Dwaah.

We are also grateful to all the people who read earlier drafts of the picture story, including members of Beverley Lewis House, Bromley Sparks, St Joseph's Specialist School and College, Tizard Centre Domestic Violence Focus Group, Researchnet Group: Linda Allchorne, Joanne Gifford, Teresa Durman, Carol Larby, Polly Sharpey, Laura Frewin, Abigail Edler, Charlotte Cranidge, Julie Anderson, Cas Anstee.

Finally we are very grateful to the Department of Health for providing financial support for this book.

Beyond Words: publications and training

Books Beyond Words will help family carers, support workers and professionals working with people who find pictures easier than words for understanding their world. A list of all Beyond Words publications, including Books Beyond Words titles, and where to buy them, can be found on our website:

www.booksbeyondwords.co.uk

Workshops about using Books Beyond Words are provided regularly in London, or can be arranged in other localities on request. Self-advocates are welcome. For information about forthcoming workshops see our website or contact us:

email: admin@booksbeyondwords.co.uk
tel: 020 8725 5512

Video clips showing our books being read are also on our website and YouTube channel: www.youtube. com/user/booksbeyondwords and on our DVD, *How to Use Books Beyond Words*.

How to read this book

There is no right or wrong way to read this book. Remember it is not necessary to be able to read the words.

1. Some people are not used to reading books. Start at the beginning and read the story in each picture. Encourage the reader to hold the book themselves and to turn the pages at their own pace.

2. Whether you are reading the book with one person or with a group, encourage them to tell the story in their own words. You will discover what each person thinks is happening, what they already know, and how they feel. You may think something different is happening in the pictures yourself, but that doesn't matter. Wait to see if their ideas change as the story develops. Don't challenge the reader(s) or suggest their ideas are wrong.

3. Some pictures may be more difficult to understand. It can help to prompt the people you are supporting, for example:

- Who do you think that is?
- What is happening?
- What is he or she doing now?
- How is he or she feeling?
- Do you feel like that? Has it happened to you/ your friend/ your family?

4. You don't have to read the whole book in one sitting. Allow people enough time to follow the pictures at their own pace.

5. Some people will not be able to follow the story, but they may be able to understand some of the pictures. Stay a little longer with the pictures that interest them.

60